"Clears Up," by Winold Reiss. From Reiss, *Six North American Indian Portrait Postcards*. © 1992 Dover Publications, Inc.

"Scalping Woman—Wife of Night Shots," by Winold Reiss. From Reiss, *Six North American Indian Portrait Postcards*. © 1992 Dover Publications, Inc.

"Lazy Boy—Blackfeet Medicine Man," by Winold Reiss. From Reiss, *Six North American Indian Portrait Postcards*. © 1992 Dover Publications, Inc.

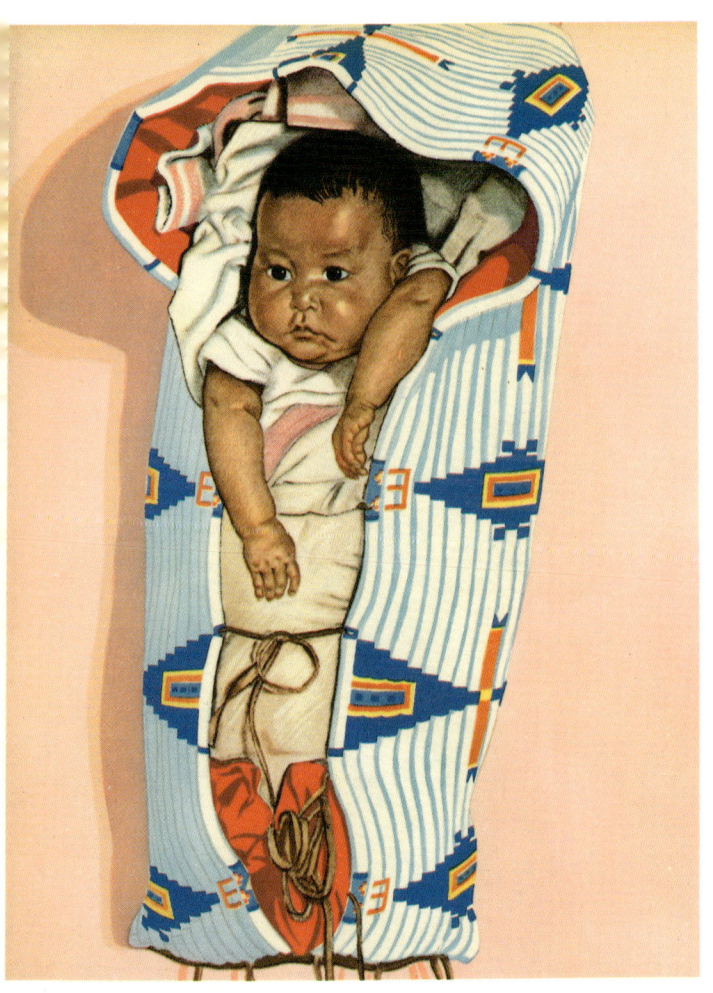

"Snow Bird—In Carrier," by Winold Reiss. From Reiss, *Six North American Indian Portrait Postcards.* © 1992 Dover Publications, Inc.

"Morning Star—Better Known as Agnes Clark," by Winold Reiss. From Reiss, *Six North American Indian Portrait Postcards.* © 1992 Dover Publications, Inc.

"Plume—A Medicine Man of the Blood Tribe," by Winold Reiss. From Reiss, *Six North American Indian Portrait Postcards*. © 1992 Dover Publications, Inc.